I Can Draw
WILD
Animals

Please visit our web site at: www.garethstevens.com
For a free color catalog describing Gareth Stevens' list of high-quality books and multimedia programs, call 1-800-542-2595 (USA) or 1-800-461-9120 (Canada). Gareth Stevens Publishing's Fax: (414) 332-3567.

Library of Congress Cataloging-in-Publication Data

Leroux-Hugon, Hélène.
   [Animaux sauvages. English]
   I can draw wild animals / by Hélène Leroux-Hugon.
     p. cm. — (I can draw animals!)
   Includes bibliographical references and index.
   ISBN 0-8368-2841-0 (lib. bdg.)
   1. Animals in art—Juvenile literature.   2. Wildlife art—Juvenile literature.
   3. Drawing—Technique—Juvenile literature. [1. Animals in art.   2. Drawing—
Technique.] I. Title.
NC780.L39313   2001
743.6—dc21   00-053145

This edition first published in 2001 by
Gareth Stevens Publishing
A World Almanac Education Group Company
330 West Olive Street, Suite 100
Milwaukee, Wisconsin 53212 USA

This U.S. edition © 2001 by Gareth Stevens, Inc. Original edition first published by Larousse-Bordas, Paris, France, under the title *Les animaux Sauvages,* © Dessain et Tolra/HER 2000. Additional end matter © 2001 by Gareth Stevens, Inc.

Illustrations: Hélène Leroux-Hugon
Photography: Cactus Studio
Translation: Valerie J. Weber
English text: Valerie J. Weber
Gareth Stevens editor: Katherine Meitner
Cover design: Katherine Kroll

Printed in the United States of America

1 2 3 4 5 6 7 8 9 05 04 03 02 01

I Can Draw

WILD Animals

Hélène Leroux-Hugon

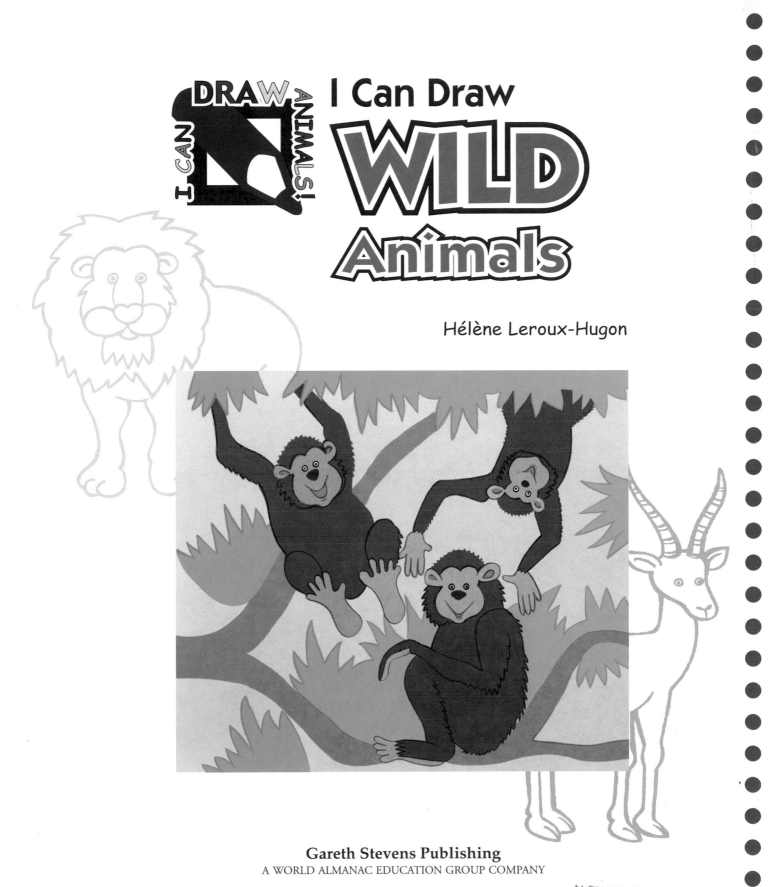

Gareth Stevens Publishing
A WORLD ALMANAC EDUCATION GROUP COMPANY

Table of Contents

I Can Draw

Observing

Before you begin, collect books and photos of African animals. If possible, visit a zoo near your home. Watch the animals, without paper or pencil. This will help you see animals in a different way. Try to find simple shapes — for example, a circle for the head or an oval for the body.

Practicing

Without a compass or stencil, draw circles, ovals, and curves by hand. This is called freestyle drawing. Notice that your circle may not be perfectly round and that an oval can be wide or narrow, short or long.

Drawing by Steps

Choose a model in the book, perhaps an elephant.

1 The elephant is made up of a large oval for the body, a smaller one for the head, and a trunk (see page 16). Step by step, draw the form with a light mark. At first, of course, your drawing is simple. This stage is called a sketch; it helps you see the size of the head compared to the size of the body and where you can accurately place each part.

2   Next, add the details like the big, beautiful ear and the little tail. Then draw the legs. Don't press too hard on your pencil because you're going to make several marks before deciding which one is the best. You will have to erase the marks shown as dotted lines on the model.

3   Finish your drawing by adding the eye and tusk. Finish the legs, toes, and slightly wavy ears. Now look at the model and redraw the outline to make the lines smoother and more lifelike. Here comes an elephant!

Now you're free to color in this drawing. You can also complete some big pictures showing several different animals and where they live.

While you are drawing, you will also learn many things about animals and their natural habitat. For example, look at the footprint left by the animal at the bottom of each page to see its shape.

Hippopotamuses

1 Draw a large oval for the body and a smaller one for the head.

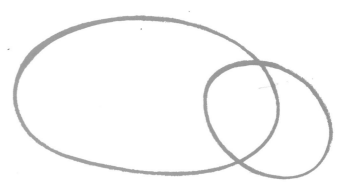

2 Redraw the shape of the head. Don't forget the huge legs and tiny ears! Erase all the dotted lines.

3 Add the eye and the nostrils, then finish the legs, hooves, and ears. Several rolls of fat at the back of the neck complete your drawing.

The hippopotamus spends most of its life in the warm, shallow waters of streams and lakes. Its baby knows how to swim before it knows how to walk. The hippopotamus can stay underwater for as long as 25 minutes without breathing!

Crocodiles

1 For the body and the head, draw a large, flat oval that is pointed at each end.

2 Draw a bump for the eye, make the mouth longer, and add a tail ready to whip the air. Begin the legs. Remember to erase the dotted lines.

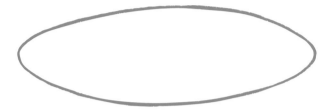

3 Look at the example, then finish your drawing by adding all the details. Don't forget the tooth that juts from its mouth!

10

The crocodile is a reptile that lives on the edge of rivers and uses its tail to swim. It eats mostly birds and fish, but it will also attack larger prey such as the gazelle and even the hippopotamus. The female lays between 20 and 90 eggs.

Ponds and Streams

In the jungles and savannas of Africa, wild animals gather at streams and ponds. Many animals come here to drink and bathe. Others come to prey upon the drinkers. The crocodile waits for a tasty fish, while the heron and the ibis catch frogs.

The Horned Rhinoceros

1 Draw two ovals — a large one for the body and a small one for the head.

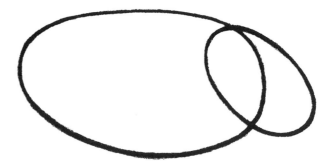

2 Now draw the ears and the famous rhinoceros horn. Begin to draw the legs. Use your eraser to rub out the dotted lines.

3 Finish drawing your rhinoceros's legs and toes. Add the tail, eye, muzzle, and mouth. Look, it is smiling at you!

14

The black rhinoceros of Africa is an herbivore. It eats bulbs and grasses. It likes to roll around in the mud, which forms a crust on its skin when it dries. While many people think the rhinoceros is a dangerous creature, it is usually quite peaceful.

15

Elephants on a Walk

1 Draw a large oval for the body, a smaller one for the head, and add a trunk.

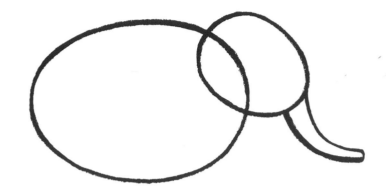

2 Draw the elephant's flapping ear and the thin tail, and begin the legs. You can also erase all the dotted lines.

3 Finish your picture by drawing the eye and the tusk. Complete the legs, toes, and slightly wavy ears.

16

The elephant eats at least 330 pounds (150 kilograms) of plants every day. It travels in herds to find enough food to eat.

While some elephants now live in reserves where they are protected, many have been killed for their ivory tusks.

The elephant is just as much fun to draw from the back or the front as from its profile. You can look at it easier this way.

The elephant is the biggest of all land animals. It has a long trunk, which is really its nose. It uses its trunk both to eat and drink.

18

It sucks in water, and then it squirts the water into its mouth. The African elephant has much bigger ears than its cousin the Asian elephant. This large jungle beast likes the little bird that cleans its thick skin and takes out many parasites.

The Giraffe Family

1 Draw a large oval for the body, two lines for the long neck, and a small oval at the end for the head.

2 Put two ears and horns on the head. Make the muzzle longer and add the mouth. Start the legs. Erase the dotted lines.

3 Look at the example, and add the details — the eyes, the nostrils, the mane, the tail, the hooves, and, of course, the spots!

The giraffe may grow to be more than 16 feet (5 meters) tall! The female gives birth to a 6-foot- (2-m-) tall baby!

The giraffe is one of few animals living on the African savanna that can eat leaves from the high branches of trees.

A Pride of Lions

1 Draw two circles, one inside the other; they will be the head and the mane. Add an oval for the body.

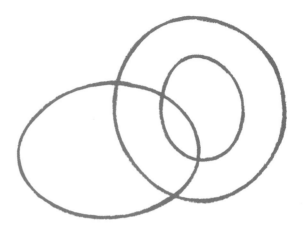

2 Change the bigger circle into a mane. Add the ears and muzzle, and begin the legs. Be sure to erase the dotted lines.

3 Look at this handsome lion and finish yours by adding the eyes, tail, paws, and all the parts of the head. See how he's looking at you?

The lion is a carnivorous animal. The females do most of the hunting in a group. They prefer to hunt animals that are young, isolated, or sick. Zebras and gazelles are easy prey for them. Females share their prey with males and cubs.

23

 Twin Gazelles

1 Draw an oval for the body, two lines for the neck, and a small oval for the head.

2 Add the horns and the ears. Begin to draw the legs. The dots show which lines you can erase.

3 Finish the delicate legs and hooves. Draw the eyes, the nostrils, the rings on the curving horns, and the stubby tail.

The gazelle lives in deserts and open plains. It has lovely horns shaped like a lyre. Gazelles travel in herds to defend themselves from predators. The gazelle's main enemies are the big cats from the African savanna — especially the lion.

The African Grasslands

On the African savanna, high grasses and baobab trees with their trunks full of water provide shade during the hottest hours of the day. Big, plant-eating mammals, such as elephants, giraffes, and zebras, live on the savanna in herds.

The number of animals in a herd depends on the weather. When it's dry, few baby animals are born. But it takes only one year of rain to help the herds get larger again.

Funny Camels

1 Draw a large oval for the body, two lines for the neck, and a small oval for the head.

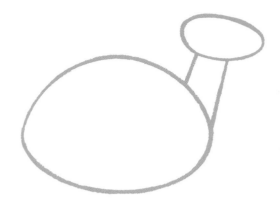

2 Draw the hump and reshape the head. Add the little ear and begin to draw the legs. Erase the dotted lines.

3 Work on the shape of the hump. (The camel only gets one!) Finish the legs and feet. Draw the eye, the muzzle, and the tail, and try to make the whole picture smoother.

The camel can live for several days without drinking water. Its single hump does not contain water, but it stores fat that allows the camel to save energy. The camel can carry people and heavy loads across the hot, sandy desert in long caravans.

The Sahara Desert

In the Sahara Desert, which covers much of northern Africa, temperatures can reach 122°F (50°C) during the day. Some animals, like the camel, the fennec, or the horned viper, have adapted well to this temperature and the lack of water.

Of all the animals living there, reptiles can stand the heat best. Plants have unusual methods of getting water. They have large root networks to absorb water anywhere they can.

The Colorful Hornbill

1 Draw a large oval for the body, two lines for the neck, an oval for the head, and the pointy beak.

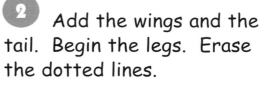

2 Add the wings and the tail. Begin the legs. Erase the dotted lines.

3 Add the casque (which looks like a hat!) on the head and the eye. Draw in the feathers of the tail and add the details. Add a small branch for it to sit on.

The hornbill lives in forests near the equator in Africa. It has a huge beak and a casque. You can see the hornbill from far away because of its bright and lively colors. Different kinds of hornbills eat different kinds of fruits and insects.

33

Silly Chimpanzees

1 Draw an oval for the body and a circle for the head.

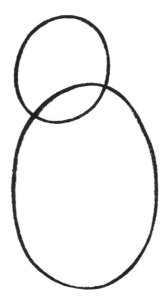

2 Start the ears and the legs. Draw the face. Erase the dotted lines.

3 Add the eyes, the nose, and the mouth. Finish the legs and paws, and draw the fur. Look! Now you have a little friend to play with you!

34

The chimpanzee is an omnivore. It eats many kinds of fruits, leaves, and insects and uses a branch to dig out termites.

Chimps are good climbers. They jump from branch to branch in the trees, where they build nests to sleep in each night.

African Rain Forests

Rain forests grow fruit and tender leaves for animals to eat all year long. They grow this food year-round because it rains there almost every day. More animal species live in these forests than anywhere else in the world.

Rain forest trees provide shelter for animals that know how to climb or fly. All kinds of monkeys such as chimpanzees and beautiful mandrills live here. You can also find pythons and other big snakes.

More to Read and View

Books about Drawing

African Animals (Kids Can Draw). Philippe Legendre (Walter Foster)

Birds of the World (Kids Can Draw). Philippe Legendre (Walter Foster)

I Can Draw That!: Easy Animals and Monsters (Books and Stuff). Robert Pierce (Grosset & Dunlap)

Learn to Draw for Ages Six and Up. Nina Kidd (Lowell House)

Mark Kistler's Imagination Station/Learn How to Draw in 3-D with Public Television's Favorite Drawing Teacher. Mark Kistler (Fireside)

Mark Kistler's Draw Squad. Mark Kistler (Fireside)

Videos

Doodle: Drawing Animals (A & F Video)

Dan Mahuta: Drawing Made Easy (A & F Video)

Web Sites

Learn to Draw with Billy Bear: www.billybear4kids.com

Draw & Color with Uncle Fred: www.unclefred.com

Some web sites stay current longer than others. To find additional web sites, enter key words based on animals and habitats you've read about in this book, such as *lion, giraffe, elephant, chimpanzee, Africa, crocodile, hippopotamus, rhinoceros,* and *savanna.*

Glossary/Index

You can find these words on the pages listed.

baobab — a tropical African tree with a swollen trunk and hard-shelled fruits. Its branches are as thick as other trees' trunks 27

caravan — a group of animals or people traveling in single file 29

carnivorous — eating the flesh of other animals 23

casque — a thick, fleshy crest that looks like a helmet on the head of some animals 32, 33

compass — a tool that helps draw circles. A compass has two arms — one placed at the center of the circle and another that holds a pencil 6

equator — the imaginary circle around the Earth located at equal distances from the North Pole and the South Pole 33

fennec — a small fox that lives in the desert, hunting at night and sleeping during the day 31

gazelle — a kind of graceful antelope with horns found in Africa and Asia 11, 23, 24, 25

habitat — the place where an animal or plant lives or grows 7

herbivore — an animal that eats plants 15

heron — a bird with a long, slim neck, a pointed bill, and long, thin legs 13

horned viper — a poisonous African snake with "horns" made from flesh that stick out over each eye 31

ibis — a wading bird with a long, slender bill 13

lyre — a musical instrument with strings 25

mammal — a warm-blooded animal that gives birth to live young 27

mandrill — a large, fierce baboon 37

muzzle — part of an animal's head, including nose, mouth, and jaws 14, 20, 22, 28

omnivore — an animal that eats both plants and other animals 35

parasite — an animal that lives on or in another animal or plant 19

predator — an animal that hunts other animals for food 25

prey — to hunt for food; also the animal that is hunted 11, 13, 23

pride — a group of lions 22

profile — a side view of a person, animal, or object 18

python — a large snake that coils around its prey and crushes it before eating 37

reptile — a cold-blooded animal with dry, scaly skin. Most reptiles reproduce by laying eggs 11, 31

reserve — an area set aside to protect animals and plants. People cannot hunt animals or gather plants in a preserve 17

savanna — a flat grassland in tropical regions 13, 21, 25, 27

species — a group of animals or plants that have certain features in common 37

stencil — a sheet of plastic or cardboard with a design cut into it used to draw specific shapes or patterns 6

termite — an insect that lives in groups and eats wood 35